CW01024073

The Weybridge Sailing Club Monologues

written and illustrated

by

T. J. Carter

ISBN 978-1-291-62470-0

This book is dedicated to

Paul Antrobus, "The Commodore"

and

all those who love the River Thames.

HKP

Hamley King Publishing
London

CONTENTS

The Tale of
Sir Peregrine Foukes

I used to iron his shirts and butter his scones.

I.

I'll tell you the tale of Sir Peregrine Foukes,
I was once his fag at Eton.
I used to iron his shirts and butter his scones
And when I didn't I was soundly beaten.

II.

In those days Sir Peregrine was a ladies' man,
A drinker, a gambler, a curser.
He made love to many a Windsor girl
And to the wife of our college bursar.

III.

The bursar's wife was a handsome woman,
Who went by the name of Kathleen.
I was in love with her myself, from afar,
And I acted as Peregrine's "go-between".

IV.

Every evening I would take Peregrine's love notes
And I would leave them in Kathleen's larder.
Then I'd watch as she went down to the
boathouse to meet him,
Glistening and heaving with ardour.

V.

She would always wear a blue velvet cape
With a hood to hide her face
And when she came back it would be all awry
From the force of his manly embrace.

VI.

She loved him true, but her love was doomed
For it was Peregrine's final year,
And he shed few tears for the bursar's wife
On the night she disappeared.

VII.

The very next day Peregrine left
To commence his army career
And they found Kathleen, without her blue cape,
Drowned in Romney Weir!

VIII.

Sir Peregrine loved the Sandhurst life,
The billiards, the claret, the porter.
He loved some ladies in Ascot too
And several in Virginia Water.

IX.

When his regiment was sent to Africa,
He said, "You know, I really don't mind,
For I'm able to leave my gambling debts
And these tiresome fillies behind!"

In African Wars Peregrine distinguished himself,
Resisting the Zulu legions,
But then he fell sick, when an infernal tick
Adhered to his nether regions.

XI.

He lay in a fever for a month or more,
You could hear the poor man yelling.
No medic was able to pull out his tick,
No nurse could ease his swelling.

The Padre tossed a Bible in his lap.

XII.

The padre tossed a bible in his lap,
Convinced he would never recover,
But the tick was bashed out by that biblical clout
And adhered to its leathery cover.

XIII.

Mistaking the bible for antelope hide,
The tick was intent on gastronomy,
But burrowing deep in the pages beneath,
It died when it reached Deuteronomy.

XIV.

When he sat up in bed, the news soon spread
Of Peregrine's miraculous survival.
He was living proof of the Church's belief
That sinners are saved by the bible.

XV.

Peregrine himself was the most impressed –
He underwent a religious conversion.
He was re-baptised in the Colonel's wife's bath,
Insisting on total immersion.

XVI.

He renounced his philandering army life.
He read the scriptures for hours.
He went home and joined a tennis club
And learned to press wild flowers.

XVII.

This new found love of tennis and floral pursuits
Was part of a Christian mission,
To invite young ladies to his country house
For chaste and earnest tuition.

XVIII.

He got a terrible crush on a Christian girl,
A wealthy Viscount's daughter,
But he never laid a finger on her nubile form,
Taking frequent showers in cold water.

XIX.

For three long years he contained himself,
After they were betrothed,
Yearning for their wedding night,
When Pamela would be unclothed.

XX.

Imagine Peregrine's disappointment
When his bride left their wedding carriage,
Making clear her religious belief
In Chastity – both before *and after* marriage.

XXI.

Locked in a loveless marriage,
Deprived of intimate relations,
Peregrine taught tennis to other young girls
To ease his seething frustrations.

XXII.

He fell madly in love with a Roedean girl
And told his wife in due course.
She looked him in the eye, and gave the steely reply,
"I don't believe in divorce!"

XXIII.

These were testing times for Peregrine
And his ardent Christianity.
He'd tried to uphold the biblical code,
But he craved some warmth and humanity.

XXIV.

They found his wife on the west walled lawn,
Face down on her artist's palette,
Nailed to the ground with a croquet hoop
And bashed on the head with a mallet.

XXV.

It was a terrible blow for Peregrine.
She must have been killed by a thief.
So he married the buxom Roedean girl,
Which helped to relieve his grief.

XXVI.

There was an Eton Old Boys' Reunion
And Peregrine went back to his college.
He'd donated a mixed doubles tennis cup
And they wanted to draw on his knowledge.

XXVII.

After the dinner was over,
He lit up a fine cigar
And wandered by the moonlit river,
Reflecting on his life so far.

XXVIII.

He came to the side of Romney Weir,
Where the weir stream leaves the river,
And, on the walkway above the surging flood,
He encountered a shadowy figure.

XXIX.

Cowled in blue velvet, the figure drew nigh,
With a face that couldn't be seen.
Peregrine's face turned ashen white,
"Can that be you Kathleen?"

XXX.

A struggle took place above the weir
As he tried to remove the cloak.
Then Peregrine slipped on some old silkweed
And the clasp on the velvet broke.

XXXI.

Peregrine slid into the torrent,
Still clinging to one half of the blue gown,
"Who are you?" he cried to the other,
"Save me or I'll drown!"

"Remember Kathleen," the other cried,
"I know it was you who drowned her!
You didn't pull her out of the weir that night,
You merciless, rotten, bounder!"

XXXIII.

"Good God! It's Carruthers!"
Yelled the drowning man,
"Come don't be cruel to Perry!
I'll spare you a thrashing if you pull me out.
You can come back to my dorm for a sherry!"

XXXIV.

The man on the weir had a change of heart.
He pulled with might and main,
But, as Peregrine emerged from the foaming
surge,
The blue velvet split in twain!

XXXV.

This time the undertow got him.
It sucked him down to drown.
He died with horror on his face
And a handful of Kathleen's gown.

XXXVI.

And how do I know of this event,
One which was seen by no others?
Because it was me who stood on the weir that
night.
Yes! I am young Carruthers!

XXXVII.

I loved Kathleen myself you know,
When I was their go-between,
And I saw Peregrine drown her
When he thought he remained unseen.

XXXVIII.

I kept her blue cloak in a box,
As a relic of that bygone age
And I went to the Eton Reunion
Full of vengeful rage.

XXXIX.

But, in the end, I tried to save him,
For the love of dear Kathleen,
For I am only a junior boy,
Their faithful go-between.

~ The End ~

The Merryman's Maid

I.

My tongue was coated in the Autumn of '88,
My hair was lank and oily,
I was mildly depressed and in need of a rest –
So I went to stay with old Dickie D'Oyly.

II.

D'Oyly Carte is a friend of mine,
I met the fellow at Cambridge.
Nowadays he lives in style on a mid-river isle,
Near the sleepy town of Weybridge.

III.

While I was huntin' and fishin',
Chasing the ladies and lovin' 'em,
D'Oyly made a fortune at the Savoy,
Managing Gilbert and Sullivan.

IV.

D'Oyly had another Cambridge chum –
The aesthetic Berrydale Fenner.
Berrydale was very thick with Sebastian Peach,
The King's College counter-tenor.

V.

Sebastian Peach would stroll by the Cam,
Hand in hand with Fenner,
Holding a lily, eating quails eggs,
And singing counter-point to his tenor.

VI.

I never much cared for Fenner and Peach,
Though they were bright and gay.
They were cruel and ambitious and some even said
They sailed the other way.
I digress…

VII.

When I arrived at D'Oyly's Island,
I surveyed his impressive mansion,
Rising out of the misty Thames,
Four miles up from Hampton.

VIII.

The bridge across was broken,
So I hailed a jovial oarsman,
Who stored his boat on Dorney Field –
This stout chap's name was Mawson.

IX.

D'Oyly came down to greet me.
He looked shaken and all of a quiver.
"Me twenty stone Soprano's broken the bridge.
She's fallen into the river!"

X.

"She's gone and lost her voice,
That warbling lump of lard,
And tomorrow's the opening night
Of *The Yeoman of the Guard*!"

XI.

Then who should appear behind him,
But the odious Berrydale Fenner.
In the intervening years he'd become
The Savoy Opera's leading tenor.

XII.

"I'm lost without my Soprano!" he sobbed,
"My diva, my lovely consort.
How can I be the star of the show,
Without her vocal support?"

XIII.

"He's in love with her," D'Oyly later on said.
"So what became of Peach?"
"Oh, his blue-eyed boy disappeared years ago,
On some Italian beach."

XIV.

"Sebastian Peach went for a swim,
Leaving his clothes on the sand.
Fenner never saw him again,
Tho' he searched for hours on that strand."

XV.

"When Fenner came back from Rome,
He became our leading tenor,
Singing with this fat soprano,
He'd found on the streets of Sienna."

XVI.

Before dinner I borrowed a boat,
Which D'Oyly moored in the reeds,
And went for a row upstream,
To Chertsey's delightful Meads.

XVII.

And there, by the water's edge,
I beheld a pastoral scene,
A Merryman in a caravan,
With a maid of seventeen.

The old Merryman, Jack, sang to her
A curious rustic song – O!
How he loved his maid, and he craved no food
And she'd leave him afore long – O!

XIX.

The Merryman's Maid returned his song,
In a voice so fresh and pretty.
I sat in my skiff in a flood of tears,
Spellbound by her ditty.

XX.

Over dinner I told D'Oyly
Of this rustic singing sensation.
Berrydale Fenner seemed strangely impressed
And asked for her Meads location.

XXI.

Drawn back to the Meads the following morn,
I found the Merryman crying,
"They came in the night and stole my maid
And now my heart is dying!"

XXII.

"One was a gent, one was a dame –
A twenty stone Italian.
They took her off to the London Savoy,
In a black trap drawn by a stallion!"

XXIII.

"Come with me!" I told poor Jack
And I hailed a passing eight.
"Row us to London," I told the cox,
"To the Savoy's embankment gate."

XXIV.

Rowing like stink, these toffs obliged.
The cox gave a mighty cheer,
When, with Jack on his lap, he hit the gap
And we cleared Teddington Weir.

XXV.

We arrived at the Savoy Opera.
We broke the backstage lock.
The fat soprano stood centre stage
In a massive "A-line" frock.

XXVI.

Her voice rang out so loud and clear,
It could be heard in Chelsea.
"That's not her that's singing," said Jack,
"That voice belongs to Elsie!"

XXVII.

We went down below the stage,
Crawling through the dirt,
Until we popped out of a little trap door,
Beneath the soprano's skirt.

a literal understudy.

XXVIII.

And there was the Merryman's Maid.
The frock was like a cuddy,
As she sang the lead part by candlelight,
A literal understudy.

XXIX.

"Elsie come back," implored poor Jack,
"Come back with me my dear".
"Be gone old fool!", the maid replied,
"This is my new career!"

XXX.

Berrydale Fenner had turned her head,
With theatrical dreams he'd impressed her.
So, in the Final Act, to win her back,
Jack went on stage as a Jester.

XXXI.

He sang his little song – O!
With all his Merryman's art,
But she rejected him from under the dress,
And he died, of a broken heart.

XXXII.

As he staggered round the stage,
In cardiac distress,
He first removed the soprano's wig
And then pulled down her dress.

XXXIII.

And there on the stage for all to see
Was no Italian lady,
But a chubby man of twenty stones,
As smooth-skinned as a baby!

XXXIV.

"My name's Sebastian Peach !" he squeaked,
His face like a red tomato,
"I've been to Rome and had the snip.
I'm opera's last Castrato!"

XXXV.

Someone threw some rotten fruit,
Two pears and a grape on.
"We paid to hear a lady sing
Not a bloomin' capon!"

XXXVI.

The air went black with flying fruit.
The crowd went white with rage.
D'Oyly bought the curtain down
To save those left on stage.

XXXVII.

"You've ruined me now," cried Fenner,
"You've dragged my name through muck.
You've just revealed, what I kept concealed,
That I sing with *a* eu-nuch!"

"How ungrateful of you," sobbed Peach,
"It's me you've humiliated,
Taking me off to that Vatican quack
To get myself castrated!"

XXXIX.

Then Fenner taunted Peach.
He really showed his claws.
"I'd rather sing with that peasant girl.
She's got a better voice than yours!"

XL.

Then Sebastian Peach brought to an end
All Fenner's singing talents.
With a twelve inch hat pin, drawn from his wig,
He stabbed him through the larynx!

XLI.

Fenner fell into the stage machinery
And now his death was certain.
When jammed, he hit a final high "C".
When crushed, he raised the curtain!

XLII.

The curtain went up and all went quiet,
For there was a little maid,
Cradling the jester in her arms
And to the audience she said…

XLIII.

"This was my friend Jack.
He died of a broken heart.
He taught me all I knew.
Now I will sing his part."

XLIV.

Then she sang the Merryman's song - O!
In a voice so fresh and pretty,
The audience sat in floods of tears
Spellbound by her ditty.

XLV.

And Gilbert turned to Sullivan
And gave his ear a bending,
"This was meant to be a comedy,
But I like this tragic ending."

And that is why, at the end
Of their *Yeoman of the Guard*,
A Merryman, for the love of his maid,
Dies of a broken heart.

~ The End ~

The Keeper of the Queen's Swans

"Take a look at my magnificent cob!"

I.

The most important man in Windsor
Was one Sir Hugh Jampton-Johns,
Liveried Grocer, Free Mason,
Keeper of the Queen's royal swans!

II.

In the third week of July,
No grander sight could be seen
Than Sir Hugh in his scarlet blazer,
"Upping" the swans for the Queen.

III.

Given Sir Hugh's sharp practices,
It came as no surprise
That the Queen's men always "upped" more
swans
Than the Vintners or the Dyers.

IV.

Sir Hugh equipped his skiff with a ramming prow,
Just like a Greek Trireme,
And, when the Vintners and Dyers greased their
rowlocks,
He put sand in their *Vaseline*!

V.

He used to lean over the swans,
So the Vintners and Dyers couldn't see
And he'd convert their one or two nicks in the
beak
To Queen Victoria's "*V*"!

VI.

Queen Victoria lost all interest in her swans
When she took to her widow's veils,
And Sir Hugh was called up to the castle one day,
By Bertie, the Prince of Wales.

VII.

"I'm taking charge of my mother's swans,"
Said the Prince, "And I've got you a special job.
Come with me to the water's edge
And take a look at my magnificent cob!"

VIII.

And there, in a golden swan-house,
With a wingspan three yards long,
Imported from the Australias,
Was the most enormous, jet-black swan!

IX.

The Prince offered Sir Hugh a cigar
And together they chewed the cud.
"I want you to guard this swan for a year –
I'm putting him out to stud!"

X.

"Find me the whitest pen that swims.
Put her in a swan-house next to the black.
Shield her from daylight for a year.
Feed her white bread through a crack."

XI.

"I'll come back to Windsor in a year.
I want to watch them mate!
Arrange me a riverside banquet.
Fatten me a goose in a crate."

XII.

"I want the finest goose in Windsor.
Feed it butter 'til it explodes.
Serve me *pâté de foie gras*
Stuffed in its parson's nose!"

XIII.

"And after this nuptial feast,
It won't be so very long
'Til we have created together
A genuine piebald swan!"

XIV.

"And when it's full grown, I'll shoot it.
As I'm royal, it's no disgrace.
And I'll be the first and only sportsman
To have such a bird in a case!"

XV.

"Here are two golden rings,
Carrying the crest of the Prince of Wales.
Use them to "mark" my black and white swans
By stapling them in their tails."

XVI.

"Do not fail me Jampton-Johns,
And you will win prestige!"
Replied the Keeper of the Swans,
"You can depend on me, my Liege!"

XVII.

Sir Hugh soon obtained the whitest of swans –
It lived on the Cliveden Reach.
And, to make it more white, soaked it overnight
In a tank of domestic bleach.

XVIII.

Sir Hugh put the gold ring in her tail
And into a swan-house she went,
Close to the house of the mighty black swan,
Who became greatly aroused by her scent!

XIX.

Unmated and deeply frustrated,
The black swan was denied her charms.
He found little relief when walked on his leash
And killed dogs and broke people's arms!

XX.

Now there was a dear little boy called Tim,
Whose Father kept the Lock at Boveney,
And one of his little legs was in irons,
Because he simply couldn't move the knee.

XXI.

Tim's pride and joy was an old grey goose,
That used to belong to his Mum.
She'd been swept away in the winter floods,
Going to the aid of her son.

One day, as Tim sat by the river,
Allowing his goose to feed,
Sir Hugh and his crew rowed into view,
With the black swan on its lead.

Arching its muscular neck,
The black swan soon broke loose
And, in spite of its daily bromide,
It tried to mate with the goose.

When the little boy fought the swan,
Its royal keeper grew irate.
He put it back on its golden lead
And stuffed the goose in a crate.

"How dare you touch a royal swan!
How dare you try to beat it!
Urchin, I'm commandeering your goose –
The Prince of Wales will eat it!"

"Urchin, I'm commandeering your goose!"

XXVI.

I, myself, was in the Queen's Boat that day.
I've "swan upped" with Sir Hugh for years.
But, to see the dismay in that little boy's face,
Moved me close to tears.

XXVII.

All that remained of that little lad's Mother
Sir Hugh had snatched away.
He'd made the royal swans his gods!
He lost my respect that day.

XXVIII.

"Row me to Windsor!" cried Sir Hugh,
"Pull and we'll soon be there.
Tonight we dine at the Masonic Lodge.
I'm being installed in the chair!"

XXIX.

I had no stomach for the Lodge that night
And, rolling back down my trouser leg,
I left Sir Hugh and his crew all shaking hands
And walked down to the river instead.

XXX.

With the help of Old Ted the Ferryman,
I rowed out to check the black swan and his mate.
How sound they slept in their golden swan-
houses,
While that poor goose was jammed in his crate.

XXXI.

And, after the Masonic Evening was over,
An inebriated Sir Hugh
Delivered the bird in the crate to the castle chef
And told him what to do.

XXXII.

Now, there was only one creature in Berkshire
More arrogant than the Prince's black cob,
And that was Betty, Sir Hugh Jampton's wife,
Who was Windsor's greatest snob!

XXXIII.

On the day of the Prince's riverside feast,
She drew up in a white feather bonnet.
Her head bore so many frills and real swan quills,
You'd think a swan were sitting upon it!

XXXIV.

When the wives of the Vintners and the Dyers
arrived,
She cried, "Get them off the Royal Barge!
They're *nouveaux riches*, so let them eat quiche
And sandwiches spread with marge!"

XXXV.

How she grovelled to the Prince of Wales.
She made sure that he sat close to her.
"My husband's the keeper of your swans,"
She said, "He's also a liveried grocer."

XXXVI.

"Spare me this small talk," grumbled the Prince,
"I haven't got all night –
Serve me my roast goose and pâté –
Then, let the black swan serve the white!"

XXXVII.

The roasted fowl delighted the Prince.
He downed it so furiously fast,
'Til all that remained was its parson's nose.
He'd saved the best bit 'til last!

XXXVIII.

"Let the mating begin!" cried the Prince,
Putting the parson's nose between his teeth.
"Open the golden gates Sir Hugh!
Let the black swan find relief!"

XXXIX.

Whooping like a moose, the black swan
Burst loose, from his golden river encampment.
As Sir Hugh and his crew clung to his leash,
He rose up like a wingéd Lion Rampant!

When the white swan failed to emerge from her
house,
There were gasps, then one or two boos,
Followed by cries of total surprise,
When out shuffled an old grey goose!

XLI..

The Prince was so shocked by this sight,
He choked on the parson's nose.
He went crimson and started convulsing
Like a man in his final death throes!

XLII.

They found the royal physician,
He was eating a left-over *hors d'oeuvre*,
And he sprang up behind the Prince
And performed the "Heinrich Manoeuvre!"

XLIII.

The parson's nose flew from his mouth.
In a soup bowl it came to rest.
And stapled in the "nose" was a golden ring,
Bearing the Prince of Wales' crest!

XLIV.

The dreadful truth dawned on the Prince,
And it didn't take very long –
He hadn't been served a goose at all.
He'd just eaten his own white swan!

XLV.

He turned on his Royal Swanherd,
His face this time purple with hate.
"You claim to be keeper of my swans,
Yet you serve them to me on a plate!"

XLVI.

Sir Hugh was mortified by these words
And down in his skiff he sat.
Then the randy black swan slipped from his grasp
And made love to his wife's feather hat!

XLVII.

With a swan bestriding her "Barnet",
Even Betty looked overawed.
She became entangled in his lead,
And her bonnet fell overboard.

"With a swan bestriding her "Barnet"."

XLVIII.

Pursuing the object of his *fétiche*,
The swan followed the hat downstream,
Dragging the wife behind him,
Of the Keeper of Swans for the Queen!

XLIX.

The royal flotilla all followed,
'Til hat and swan went over a weir,
And, when his wife got jammed on the weir frame,
Sir Hugh rowed alongside to see her.

L.

"Husband, give me a knife to cut the leash,
Or down in the weir pool I'll go!"
"My dear, I'm the keeper of that swan,"
Said Sir Hugh, "So I'm afraid the answer's 'No!'"

LI.

Chafed on the weir frame, the swan's leash
snapped
And out of the river the angry wife rose.
And, grabbing hold of Sir Hugh's swan-upper's
knife,
She cut several nicks in his nose!

LII.

The arguing couple were cast adrift in an oar-less
skiff.
They looked so common and scruffy.
The Vintners and the Dyers jeered them both
And pelted them with their buffet.

LIII.

And what became of the randy black swan
The Prince never realised.
Following the hat into a paddle steamer's blades,
It got itself liquidised!

LIV.

And the only person who cared
To look upstream that day was me.
And I saw Old Ted the Ferryman,
Rowing little Tim's goose back to Boveney!

LV.

You see, on the night of the Masonic do,
It was me and dear Old Ted,
Who put the goose into the swan-house
And the swan in the goose-crate instead.

LVI.

And that's the tragedy of Sir Hugh Jampton-Johns,
Who was once the Keeper of the Queen's Royal
Swans.
He caused the Prince to eat his pen.
He lost his cob and failed to catch it...

… He was driven from Windsor in disgrace
And lived the rest of his life in Datchet!

~ The End ~

The Oxford Cox

"You can't bring along your Butler!"

I.

I'll tell you the tale of the Oxford Cox,
The most beautiful youth, with golden locks.
It was in the year I first met Deborah,
And rowing "Four" in our boat was dear Lord
Desborough.

II

Lord Desborough was a tremendous sportsman
And not just at games with balls.
He could fence and hunt, row and punt
And twice swam Niagara's Falls!

III.

He was Captain of Rowing at Oxford
That year (1877), but here came the rub –
Apart from me, the rest of the crew were
Members of the Debag'em Club!

IV.

The Debag'em Club met once a month
To trash their college quarters,
To debag poor chaps from other halls
And to throw bread rolls at the porters!

V.

The Chairman of the Debag'em Club
Was the infamous Lord Bunny Stoat.
The problem for dear old Desborough
Was that Stoat was the Oxford Stroke.

VI.

Roger Smoothly rowed at "Two".
His behaviour was quite obscene:
He'd seduced some thirty blue-stocking girls
And the wife of the Brasenose Dean!

VII.

The Oxford Cox was a man called Brown.
He'd bring aboard the hampers.
He couldn't steer the boat at all,
But he'd ply the crew with champers.

VIII.

The Oxford Cox would shave the Stroke,
And supervise his pets,
And sometimes he would go ashore
To place Stoat's gambling bets.

IX.

One day on the river at Oxford,
Practising for the Varsity Race,
Lord Desborough suddenly shouted,
"This is a total disgrace!"

X.

"Listen Stoat, I'm sacking Brown.
I don't know how to make this subtler.
If you want to be Stroke in the Oxford boat,
You can bring along your butler!"

XI.

"I'm getting another cox today.
I don't care who he is!
I'll recruit the first fellow who comes along –
He's got to steer better than this!"

XII.

I've never seen Desie so angry before.
His 'tache was all of a quiver.
His eyes scanned the horizon for another cox,
As we meandered up the river.

XIII.

And there, on Folly Bridge,
Above the Christ Church Meadow,
Sat a beautiful girl on a strange machine,
Also mounted by a dull-looking fellow.

XIV.

"What a beautiful filly!" said Roger,
Waving to the maiden and leering.
"She's with some pleb from Trinity Hall,
Where they let 'em read engineering!"

XV.

"The name and purpose of your machine?"
Shouted Desborough, "I want to understand 'em."
"My name's Maurice Boote," came the reply,
"And this is a proto-type tandem."

XVI.

"My friend Deborah sits behind me –
She reads Classics and Cardinal Newman.
We're both in the Oxford Movement –
In fact we're off to Holy Communion."

XVII.

"Don't mind me saying, but your steering was out
When you rowed upriver to Folly.
I've some ball-race pullies I could fit to your boat.
I designed them for Fletcher's Trolley."

XVIII

So Desborough made this Maurice Boote the cox,
Ignoring Stoat and Smoothly's scoffs.
And, in spite of those Debag'em toffs,
Our speed increased by several knots.

XIX.

We became Boat Race favourites with Boote
aboard.
Yet Stoat treated him ever-so rudely.
What worried Boote more was the amount of time
His Deborah was spending with Smoothly.

"I don't need a ride home, Maurice."

XX.

After training she'd always say to Boote,
"I don't need a ride home Maurice.
I've been invited back to Roger's rooms
To read the Odes of Horace!"

XXI.

It was the day before the Boat Race
And the Debag'ems were in the bath.
I was in an adjoining room,
Waxing my manly moustache.

XXII.

Desborough had left early that day
To catch the London train,
When I heard the voice of Bunny Stoat,
Echoing out of the drain.

XXIII.

"Chums, unless I clear my gambling debts
And do so sooner than later,
The Brasenose Dean'll send me down
And I'll be cut off by Pater."

XXIV.

"So I've placed a thousand guinea bet
To clear my debts complete.
I've a hundred-to-one on Oxford
To win by *exactly five feet.*"

XXV.

"We'll overtake Cambridge at Barnes,
But we mustn't over-perform.
If our lead increases by more than five feet,
We'll dose Desborough with chloroform."

XXVI.

"We need to get another cox,
Who'll let us do as we like.
We must get rid of Boote 'n' his girl.
We'll nobble them in Putney tonight!"

XXVII.

"We need to grease the Umpire's palm.
So that in a close decision he helps.
We'll meet him tonight in 'The Olde Spotted
Horse' –
His name is 'Honest John' Phelps."

XXVIII.

So shocked was I to hear this plot.
It must not run its course.
I took the train to Putney
And entered "The Olde Spotted Horse".

XXIX.

I took up station in a snug,
Commanding a saloon bar vista,
And watched Stoat greet the Umpire,
Through the leaves of an aspidistra.

XXX.

Stoat plied "Honest John" with liquor,
And slipped him a sizeable bung,
Made him repeat "By exactly five feet"
And loaded his starting-gun.

XXXI.

Then into the pub ran Maurice Boote,
In dishevelled and frantic mode.
"Smoothly's abducted my Deborah!" he cried,
"To a mansion in Werter Road!"

XXXII.

"Let's investigate," said Stoat,
Pocketing the Umpire's gun,
"This drunken oaf has fallen asleep.
Come with me Maurice, run!"

XXXIII.

As Stoat and Maurice left the pub,
In came dear Lord Desborough.
"Stoat's trying to fix the race," I said,
"They've gone to look for Deborah."

XXXIV.

Then Stoat and Smoothly entered the pub,
With a youth with golden locks.
"Boote and his girl have disappeared,"
Said Stoat, "I've found us another cox."

XXXV.

"This golden youth's from Teddy Hall –
I believe his name is Ned."
"He'll have to do," said Desborough,
"For I am off to bed."

XXXVI.

The next morning at Putney Bridge,
No sign of the Umpire was seen.
So young Ned both coxed and started the race
And we powered away upstream.

XXXVII.

"Stop the race!" came a cry from Putney Bridge.
"Restart it or abandon!"
It was "Honest John" Phelps the Umpire,
On the back of Maurice Boote's tandem.

XXXVIII.

"This is the Oxford Cox," shouted Phelps,
"I found him bound in a Putney shed."
"What have you done with my Deborah?"
Cried Boote, "I fear she may be dead!"

XXXIX.

How the crowd thrilled to the race.
They'd never seen the like:
Two crews in pursuit on the river,
Pursued by two men on a bike!

XL.

Stoat winked at the Cox below Barnes
And the Oxford crew drew level.
On the bank the Umpire fell from the bike,
His turn-up caught in a pedal.

XLI.

Debag'em cads caught up with Boote
And tore his trews asunder.
He was thrown off Barnes Bridge on his bike,
Just as the crews went under!

XLII.

Our boats emerged from 'neath the bridge
To thunderous applause.
We matched each other stroke for stroke,
With our eight remaining oars.

XLIII.

"Let's take 'em now," cried Stoat,
"And remember it's by five!"
But we couldn't gain an inch on them,
No matter how we tried.

XLIV.

"Honest John" Phelps was in a launch,
When we crossed the finish line.
Bunny Stoat's butler had picked him up
And got him there on time.

XLV.

Desborough and I were desolate.
We would have accepted defeat.
But "Honest John" Phelps pronounced: "A draw –
To Oxford – by *exactly five feet!*"

XLVI.

Stoat and Smoothly punched the air.
The Debag'em Club all cheered.
"This cannot stand. They've fixed the race,"
Protested young Ned, who'd steered.

XLVII.

"You know too much," cried Stoat,
"You'll bring us to perdition!"
Then he threw the Cox into the Thames,
In keeping with tradition.

The smoke cleared ......

.....Desborough was still standing!

XLVIII.

The young cox started to drown,
As soon as he left the boat.
Desborough sprang to his feet to save him,
But was shot in the chest, by Stoat.

XLIX.

The smoke cleared – Desborough was still
standing –
No hint of blood on his manly Bristol.
The gun, brought afloat from his coat by Stoat,
Was the Umpire's starting-pistol!

L.

"You'll get sent down for this!"
Said Des, before diving into the tide
And swimming after the drowning cox,
Using both Trudgen stroke and side.

LI.

The Cox was face down when Des reached him.
His lungs were all out of air.
Desborough towed him to the Middlesex bank,
Holding onto his golden hair.

LII.

I knelt with Desborough beside the youth:
His knees were smooth, not knobbly,
And, when I went to rub his chest,
It felt so strangely wobbly!

LIII.

And, when the Cox opened his eyes,
It dawned on me and Desborough
That the Oxford Cox wasn't a chap –
She was the missing Deborah!

LIV.

"Give her a lengthy kiss of life,"
Said Des, "As I'm not qualified.
I'll settle with Cambridge for the draw,
Before we're disqualified."

LV.

Stoat and Smoothly tried to sneak off,
While the Umpire did his report make,
But the Cambridge crew debagged 'em both
And threw 'em off the bank at Mortlake.

LVI.

An hour after the race was over,
Maurice Boote swam ashore,
And he explained to me and Desborough
How the race had been a draw.

LVII.

"There's always an explanation",
He said, "Of events that might seem random.
When I was thrown off the bridge at Barnes,
The boats went through the wheels of my
tandem."

LVIII.

"So they couldn't pass each other.
They were dead level all the time.
You'll find the prows stapled together,
By my bike, 'neath the Plimsoll line."

LIX.

"I'll retrieve our cycle Deborah.
Then I'll give you a lift back home."
"I'm very sorry", said the Oxford Cox,
"But now you must cycle alone."

LX.

"You see...
With Roger, I discovered the tragedies of
Euripides,
I explored the Odes of Horace.
I can't spend my life with nuts 'n' bolts,
And an engineer, called Maurice."

LXI.

"I need you, Maurice," said Desborough, "for I
Got a thousand-to-one on the draw with
Cambridge.
I could do with a first class engineer –
I'm going to straighten the river at Weybridge."

LXII.

And this is why…

Whenever I row the Thames at Weybridge,
I think so fondly of Desborough,
But more fondly still of the Oxford Cox,
For 'twas I who married Deborah!

~ The End ~

The Painted Sparrow

He ended up painting a sparrow!

I.

Young Johnny Jones lived near Lechlade,
His mother worked at the Mill.
Johnny was her pride and joy –
She knew the lad was ill.
She worked the wool for Johnny.
He was her hope and her dream.
But she slipped one day at Filkins Mill,
And fell in a fulling machine.

II.

Johnny's Aunt had perished too,
As she nursed him through that winter.
She rested her hand on his rustic cot,
And picked up a fatal splinter.

III.

So all Johnny had was his Uncle Jim,
Who used to sit and drink.
He'd say, "Young John, we need a song,"
Then he'd stare in his gin and think.

IV.

"I have it!" he cried to Johnny one day,
Whose expression never seemed to vary,
"I know a breeder in Enstone –
I'll buy you a singing canary!"

V.

His intentions were clear when he set out,
But they became less clear in "The Harrow".
The canary idea got drowned in Jim's beer,
And he ended up *painting a sparrow*!

VI.

Now this might seem a shabby deed,
But Uncle's thoughts were kind.
He'd once painted the angels in Lechlade Church
And had yellow paint left behind.

VII.

And how Johnny loved his little bird,
That dear little painted thing.
"You've given me something to live for," he said:
"I'll teach my canary to sing.
I'll teach him the songs the angels sing –
I heard them once at the Church.
Then he can sing them for you and for me,
When he's sitting at home on his perch."

VIII.

The good people of St. Lawrence
Whispered at Evensong:
"Who is that solemn little boy
Who hasn't been coming long?"
"Why does he listen quite so hard?"
"Why does he talk to his hat?"
"What is it that he keeps in a piece of wool,
Wrapped up in the lining of that?"

"How can he sit so easily
On a pew so hard and narrow?"
"What's that chirping noise tonight?
Aaah, p'rhaps 'tis only some sparrow."

IX.

Johnny went to church alone
When Sunday evenings came.
His Uncle sat in the grate at home
And hung his head in shame.
"I've been a drunkard all my life –
I've always been the same.
That sparrow will never sing," he wept,
"And I'm the one to blame!
That poor little mite goes off to church,
With a sparrow in his hat.
I've never heard a sparrow sing,
Only a sparrow chat.
The young lad's borne so many blows,
But this is the cruellest yet –
He hasn't got a canary at all,
And 'twas I who painted his pet!"

X.

He sat in the grate with a bottle o' gin –
Oh, see what gin can do!
He was covered in soot and soaked to the skin,
For 'twas raining down the flue.
He'd made the devil drink his god,
And ruined his clothing too!

XI.

But, if he'd cleaned himself up and gone to church
He'd have witnessed a wonderful thing.
For a little bird, wrapped in a piece of wool,
Had suddenly learned to sing.

XII.

Was it the love of a little boy
Whose soul was free from taint?
Was it the sparrow's exceptional skill,
Or something in the paint?
'Twas in the "Old One Hundred",
It slowly dawned on the choir –
Another voice was singing,
Higher and more inspired.
It started off quite piano,
But soon grew clear and strong,
With a range far beyond the soprano,
Who'd been in the choir too long.

XIII.

The congregation turned as one,
And beheld a little fellow,
With a singing bird in the palm of his hand,
Painted canary yellow.

They thrilled to the sound of the little bird,
As he trilled with feathers puffed.
Even the parson was greatly impressed,
And offered to have it stuffed.

With a singing bird in the palm of his hand—

XIV.

Young Johnny stood with a trembling hand,
Smiling though his tears.
'Twas the first time he'd ever smiled
In all his tender years.

Tears of pride and joy they were –
They drove away his fears.
He'd taught his little bird to sing!
The congregation cheered!

XV.

As John went home 'cross Ha'penny Bridge,
Where Thames' sweet waters swirled,
He saw heavenly clouds clothe the spire,
And all seemed right with the world.

XVI.

This should have been the ending,
The rightful happy end,
To the tale of Johnny Jones
And his yellow feathered friend.
They should have lived a life
Of song and joy and laughter.
They should have lived a life
Of happy ever after.
They should have lived a life
Where to hear a sparrow sing,
Was something much more highly prized
Than guzzling bottles of gin…

But, even as they fell asleep,
Uncle stirred in the grate.
He crawled about and craved for gin,
His raging thirst to slake.
He poured himself a pint of gin.
He looked for ice and lemon.
He lifted down the old fruit bowl –
There was only half a melon.
With bleary eyes he spied the bird –
He thought it was a lemon!
And Johnny Jones' sparrow,
In yellow-painted trim,
Was cast away like a piece o' fruit,
And drowned in a pint of gin!

He thought it was a lemon!

XVIII.

And that's the way it's always been,
Since the world's inception –
Our golden dreams are washed away,
Our heaven-sent dreams of perfection.

XIX.

I still attend St. Lawrence Church –
I do as I did then,
But there's a little boy I knew
Who's never come again.
And, when I hear the old Church choir,
At the ending of the day,
I hear them sing their evening hymn,
But, inwardly, I say…

XX.

"Put down your ancient psalters!
Yes, close those dusty tomes!
You'll never sing to me sweet psalmody,
Like the sparrow o' Johnny Jones."

"'Twas only a trill – I remember it still –
'Tis fixed in my heart like an arrow!
'Twas only the song of a poor boy's bird,
The song of a painted sparrow!"

~ The End ~

The Maidenhead Cheese

Passing crews.... veered from the windward in shock!

I.

"Four men in a boat. What a grand idea!"
Said George, "It'll cure Jerome's diseases."
Then Harris said, "Tom, will you come along?"
And I said, "Yes, I'll bring my two cheeses!"

II.

"Cheese in a boat is a bad idea",
Said Jerome, "It's impossible to keep it cool.
I've travelled with Tom's dreadful cheeses before,
On a train back from Liverpool."

III.

"I can't leave the cheeses at home," I said,
"On account of their powerful smell.
My wife and children have had to move out
To live in a local hotel."

IV.

So it was decided: *three* men would go
In the boat and they'd take a *dog* instead.
I would try to get rid of my cheeses.
Then, I'd meet them in Maidenhead.

V.

The public mortuary refused my cheeses –
So I wrapped them up and took 'em –
In a cheese-cloth sack, on the luggage rack
Of an empty train to Cookham.

VI.

I punted downstream from Cookham,
For they were draining Boulter's Lock.
Passing crews who got a whiff of my cargo
Veered from the windward in shock!

VII.

I left my two cheeses moored in my punt,
Just where the Cliveden Reach dwindles,
And proceeded on foot past the drained-out lock
To a Thameside Hotel called "Skindles".

VIII.

The Landlord of "Skindles" stood by the door.
He was dressed in a nautical manner.
Known to all as "The Commodore",
He had a big-chested daughter called Anna.

IX.

River swells and their gels crammed the 'otel,
But the Lord of all he could see
Was a conceited dandy who sat, sipping brandy,
With big Anna upon his left knee.

X.

"Anna my dear!" he sang in her ear,
"You rouse me to heights of affection,
Come upstairs to my suite of rooms,
And I'll show you my stamp collection!"

XI.

You could see from the Commodore's face
That he didn't like the scenario
And, when his daughter got dragged upstairs,
I asked him: "Who's the Lothario?"

XII.

"His name is John, but they call him 'Sir John' –
He's descended from the rakish George Villiers.
He's renting Spring Cottage near
Cliveden House. *[sniffs]*
Your strange cologne, sir, is making me bilious!"

XIII.

Sir John had a valet who told me more.
He said, "My own name is Reg,
I write all Sir John's conquests in this book –
In bed, he's a living 'ledge!'"

XIV.

"There's four score from Windsor, and twenty
from Henley –
Look, here is a list of their names.
There's one Weybridge lady, but thirty from
Chertsey
And a hundred and eighty from Staines!"

XV.

"Don't leave me, Sir John!" wept Lady Vera,
"Don't you remember your vows and mine?"
" 'Course he remembers," called out the valet,
"You're here in his book at four thousand and
nine!"

XVI.

"Save me!" cried Anna, from a room above,
And the Commodore ran to her aid.
But the rampant John had already moved on,
Along with Christine, a randy barmaid.

XVII.

"After him!" shouted the Commodore,
With weeping women in tow.
As he passed I asked to rent a room –
He sniffed me, and answered, "No!"

XVIII.

I returned to my punt as darkness fell.
I felt alone and so forlorn,
As I moored that craft on a Cliveden isle,
Midstream near the Spring Cottage lawn.

XIX.

I attempted to drown my cheeses,
But they both floated in the water.
So I cut one of the two in four
And successfully ate a quarter.

XX.

I fell into a deep and troubled sleep,
But, just as I started to dream,
I was roused from my island slumbers
By a woman's piercing scream.

XXI.

"My father's been hurt by Sir John!
He's bashed him on the head!
He's run him through with a rapier!
I fear he may be dead!"

XXII.

'Twas Anna, the Commodore's daughter,
A body lay on the lawn,
A figure ran off through Cliveden Woods,
With moonlit rapier drawn.

XXIII.

"You didn't see a thing!" said Reg,
When, much to my surprise,
The valet appeared on my island
And shone a torch into my eyes.

XXIV.

I thought it was best not to argue
With one of a brace of felons,
Who then went on to eat half a cheese,
Saying: "It smells, faintly, of melons."

XXV.

"I'll take the other cheese to Sir John,"
Said Reg, "but, if he doesn't like,
I'll weigh it down in Boulter's Lock –
They're refilling it tonight!"

XXVI.

Half an hour went past and, still aghast,
I was pouring myself a toddy
When Reg dragged a sack down the far bank
Which appeared to contain a body.

XXVII.

I ate the remaining quarter of cheese,
But, just as I was falling asleep,
Every light came on in great Cliveden House –
So I crept up through the woods to peep.

XXVIII.

An eighteenth century ball was on.
Every guest held a grotesque mask.
And, though they all wore powdered wigs,
I soon recognised the cast.

XXIX.

Sir John was dressed as a foppish Duke.
Reg was a footman, like Dandini.
Vera a countess, with maid Christine,
And yet none of 'em seemed able to see me.

Yet none of them seemed able to see me!

XXX.

Then Sir John and Reg exchanged their clothes,
So that Vera thought Reg was Johnny,
While the real Sir John made off with her maid
For a touch of "Hey-nonny-nonny!"

XXXI.

Then Anna burst in with a military guard,
Who seized and unmasked the flunky.
"The organ grinder's escaped," said Reg,
"You've only arrested his monkey!"

XXXII.

"He's probably gone down to Maidenhead –
He's a maid there and he's fond of 'er."
When the guards rushed off, Reg left too,
But *upstream*, in a gondola.

XXXIII.

I punted a little way behind,
As Reg plied that magnificent craft.
He moored near Cookham Churchyard
And I followed him up the path.

XXXIV.

By an imposing tomb he met Sir John,
Who slapped him upon the back.
John took back his clothes and laughed and sang,
Drinking sherry from a sack.

XXXV.

John lent on the statue of a man,
Who had died in years of yore.
Then, I noticed its white marble features
Were those of the Commodore!

XXXVI.

Suddenly the statue moved its head
And its stone-cold lips as well.
"Sir John! Sir John! Repent!" it roared,
"Or I'll drag you down to Hell!"

XXXVII.

Sir John finished drinking his sherry
And stuck the sack on the statue's head.
"Join me for supper, if you like!"
He sang, "For we're cruising to Maidenhead!"

XXXVIII.

I watched them cruise to Boulter's Lock,
Under the moonlight shining.
Gondolier Reg was sculling astern,
John ate supper reclining.

XXXIX.

What happened next I will never forget –
Oh, it haunts my sleepless nights –
What occurred in that drained-out lock chamber,
'Neath the workmen's dismal lights.

"Sir Johnny! I have come to you for supper!"
There came the most infernal roar —
Down in the lock, with a sack on his head,
Stood the statue of the Commodore!

Sir John went down to meet his guest —
They were ankle deep in water.
"Repent Sir John! You murdered me!"
It roared, "You ravished my only daughter!"

"It was only a bit of fun," sang John,
"And for your mercy, I won't beg."
So the statue slammed shut the downstream sluice,
And it trapped Sir John, by the leg.

Demonic workmen refilled the lock.
Foaming waters flooded the chamber.
"Throw me a mallet," John called to his valet,
"I'm in a spot of danger."

Sir John smashed the head off the statue!

XLIV.

Sir John smashed the head off the statue!
It sank in the lock in its sack.
The water was up to John's chin by now,
And his bottle was starting to crack.

XLV.

"I'm only guilty of *love*," he sang,
"As five thousand women will tell.
I was trying to find 'Little-Miss-Right' –
Don't drag me down to Hell!"

XLVI.

I shall never forget his dying song,
It was heard from near and far.
As he went to Hell in a lock chamber,
He let out a plaintive, "Aaaah!"

XLVII.

And then Jerome woke me up.
"You're asleep in your punt," he said.
"Join the three of us and the dog,
When we row out of Maidenhead."

XLVIII.

"The types you get in Maidenhead,"
He said, "Have always played fast and loose!
Today they're re-draining the lock again,
For something's jammed in the sluice."

XLIX.

They re-drained the lock in front of a crowd.
The Lock Keeper was furious.
Rumours had spread of what I'd seen –
All of Maidenhead was curious.

L.

They found the cause of the blockage,
Wedged in the sluice gate's trap.
It wasn't just the usual old boot,
But a large object in a sack.

LI.

The Lock Keeper went down in the lock.
The crowd gathered round to see.
"The Keeper's going to cut open the sack –
What can that object be?"

LII.

The assembled throng shrank back as one.
Cries of horror filled the air.
For, when he opened the sodden sack,
He found... my Camembert!

LIII.

"You must have eaten one cheese yourself,"
Said Jerome, "You knew it would revolt us.
Then you put the second in the empty lock,
Before falling asleep near Boulter's."

LIV.

"And, as for the rest, you dreamed it all.
I find your story quite abhorrent.
You're a chap with whom cheese disagrees.
You may be lactose intolerant!"

LV.

"Let's get out of Maidenhead –
Then we'll all feel cheered.
We can't get rooms at 'Skindles'
Because the Landlord's disappeared".

LVI.

The three men in a boat rowed off,
As happy as you please.
And I was left alone once more,
In my punt, with a piece of cheese.

LVII.

As I punted past Spring Cottage,
A chap was cutting the hedge.
"Hello, old friend!" he shouted out,
"Remember me, I'm Reg!"

LVIII.

"Sir John didn't want your cheese,"
Said Reg, "It always makes him dream.
So I weighed it down in the lock last night,
While John played in the pool with Christine."

LIX.

"So it *must* have all been a dream," I thought,
But I punted as fast as I could,
When I thought I saw Anna leading the police
Down through the Cliveden Wood.

LX.

And Cliveden House looked different now,
But what alarmed me more:
The house I'd seen had been burnt down,
One hundred years before!

LXI.

I never looked for the headless statue
When I left the Cliveden Reach.
I took my cheese to Eastbourne
And buried it on the beach.

And this is why …

LXII.

Weak- chested people went to Eastbourne
And many still go there –
To stroll along the lovely prom
And to breathe the fortified air.

LXIII.

And the moral of my story's this:
If you want a life of ease –
Avoid the Thames at Maidenhead
And eating too much cheese!

~ The End ~

Epilogue

Weybridge Sailing Club
The Golden Years

I.

For fifty years this Sailing Club
Has stood beside the Thames,
Half concealed in Dorney Field,
Where the river bends.

II.

For fifty years it's welcomed Weybridge folk
To make this place their home.
It matters not if they can't sail,
Or if they come from Addlestone!

III.

Weybridge sailors sometimes rig their boats,
And sail them up and down.
But they're happiest of all at anchor,
In the back bar of "The Crown".

IV.

There's a very fine sailing club downsteam,
But, to me, the heart of this little club is bigger.
For we have a love that money can't buy,
We're bonded by our love of that river.

V.

And on the day they lay me to rest,
I hope that heaven will be
Like a sunny day on the Thames,
Among Weybridge friends,
At dear old W.S.C.

VI.

And here on Earth, in the years ahead,
Whatever might occur,
May God bless Weybridge Sailing Club,
And all who sail in her!

~ The End ~

Performance Notes

In General

The monologues are designed to be performed after a dinner, with wine, which you, yourself, are attending. So, keep props to a minimum (a hat will normally suffice) and make sure there is a relatively temperate prompter at your table. It adds to the entertainment if you coarsely act out the moments of high drama while you are reciting: e.g. boat races, swan attacks, murders, seductions, fights on top of weirs or at the bottom of locks, etc. If the monologue features several characters, give these differing, easily recognisable accents or physical mannerisms, so that a well wined-and-dined audience can distinguish between them more readily. Good luck!

The Tale of Sir Peregrine Foukes

This monologue was first performed at the W.S.C. Annual General Meeting held at "The Ship Hotel", Weybridge on the 31st of January 2010. The only prop required is a good quality smoking hat, which should be solemnly placed on the head before the recitation begins. (Lock & Co. Hatters, St. James' Street, London, have an excellent "Fez and Smoking Hat" section.)

The Merryman's Maid

This monologue was first performed at the W.S.C. Annual General Meeting held at "The Ship Hotel", Weybridge on the 6th of February 2011. Again, the only prop required is a smoking hat. In verses 34 and 38, Sebastian Peach should speak in a loud falsetto voice.

The Keeper of the Queen's Swans

This monologue was first performed at the W.S.C. Annual General Meeting held at "The Warren Lodge Hotel", Shepperton on the 5th of February 2012.

A different hat is required for this monologue as worn by the Keeper of the Swans. Adapt a "Captain" style boating hat (often favoured by Thames pleasure cruiser skippers) by putting a badge featuring a swan and/or royal crest on it. Stick a swan's feather at a jaunty angle in the hat band behind the badge. (A goose quill will do if you can't find a real swan's feather.)

N.B. Verse 5 should be amended if you have some real, knowledgeable "swan-uppers" in your audience. The "V" is actually the mark of the Vintners, and *not* Queen Victoria, whose mark was two horizontal "nicks" above three vertical. The amended verse 5 should read: "And he'd convert their one or two nicks in the beak, To Victoria's 'Two-b'-Three'".

The Oxford Cox

This monologue was first performed at the W.S.C. Annual General Meeting held at "The Warren Lodge Hotel", Shepperton on the 3rd of February 2013.

The hat required for this monologue is a 'retro' rowing cap with the Oxford University crest upon it. Also wear an Oxford rosette and a small, but dapper, stick-on moustache. One other prop is carried in the pocket: a referee's whistle.

Verse 45: The whistle is produced and blown when the Umpire gives his unusual verdict at the end of the race: "But 'Honest John' Phelps pronounced [*whistle*] 'A draw – To Oxford – by exactly five feet!'".

Distinguishing the characters: Maurice Boote, the tandem-riding engineer, should speak in a Midlands accent or Peter Cook's E.L. Wisty voice. "Honest John" Phelps, the Umpire, should speak in a 1970's shop steward/police constable voice. Lord Bunny Stoat should speak very quickly, affecting a foppish "tea-pot" stance, which he reverses after each statement. Deborah should speak in a slow, sanctimonious voice. Lord Desborough should be portrayed as a fine, upstanding decent chap, which he was, of course, in real life.

The Painted Sparrow

This monologue was first performed at the W.S.C. Annual General Meeting held at "The Warren Lodge Hotel", Shepperton on the 1st of February 2009.

The only prop required is a smoking hat. This is the most tragic of the monologues, and should be performed with serious sincerity. Don't be surprised if your performance evokes tears more than laughter.

The Maidenhead Cheese

This monologue is to be performed at the W.S.C. Annual General Meeting to be held at "The Warren Lodge Hotel", Shepperton on the 26th of January 2014.

A straw boater hat *and* an eighteenth century powdered wig are the required props for this piece as there is a time shift in the narrative from before to after the narrator's eating of the strong cheese and, again, when its (apparent) effect wears off. Begin the monologue wearing the boater hat. At the end of verse 27, remove the boater and place the wig upon your head. The wig stays in place until the end of verse 46. The boater is put back on, replacing the wig, just before the line: "And then Jerome woke me up".

Characterisation: Sir John's lines (verses 10, 37, 42, 43, 45) should be *sung* in a cod-operatic voice. In verse 46, Sir John's final cry of "Aaaah!" should be cut off at the end by a glugging sound because he is, in fact, going down to Hell, by drowning. The only other sung line belongs to the Commodore and comes at the beginning of verse 40: "Sir Johnny! I have come to you for supper!" should be delivered in a terrifying "hearse-like" *basso profundo*. Reg, Sir John's valet, should speak in a 1970's shop steward/police constable voice. Jerome, in spite of his well-deserved comic reputation, should be played as a rather serious and sensible person.

Weybridge Sailing Club – The Golden Years

This little poem was first performed in Dorney Field, among the boats, on the 7th of July 2012 as the climax to a rambling sermon given by the Club Chaplain (dressed in full clerical garb) on the occasion of W.S.C.'s Golden Jubilee Regatta.

Acknowledgements

I would like to acknowledge my dear wife, Jenny, who clarified and incorporated the illustrations, formatted the text and designed the cover. Without Jenny's very talented assistance this book would not have been published. My thanks are due, also, to my helpful researcher, Mrs Shirley Egan; my colleague, Mrs Ayesha Sodhi, who kindly typed the manuscript; my brother, Daniel Carter, who proof-read the typescript and my trusty prompter, Miss Lizzi Willcocks.

I would like to thank all those who have inspired, encouraged or listened to the monologues over the years, in particular: Rodney and Pat Agambar, Paul and Angie Antrobus, Evelyn Ashworth, Derek Benelisha, Pat, John and Eric Brewer, David Bridel, Nick and Eleanor Butler, Nel Campbell (née Brown), Joseph and George Carter, Cameron Christie, Ian Curtis, Lorenzo da Ponte, Neil and Sue Davey, Anders and Clare Eklund, W.S. Gilbert, Phil and Jackie Gray, Mike Hall, Nick and Medy Hart, Roy Hathaway, J. Milton Hayes, Hugh and Hannah Hefferland, Linda Henry, Jerome K. Jerome, Eric Matthews, Ian and Liz Mawson, Tony and Angela O'Leary, David Orme, Tom and Mary Phillips, Andrew ("Stan") Stanley and Hieromonk Theophan Willis ("Ken").

Finally, I would like to acknowledge my dear friend and mentor in the "Art of Coarse Acting", the Reverend Martin Hussey. In 1974 Martin supplied me with two pages of one-line pantomime jokes. Among them was a joke which led me to conceive the tale of *The Painted Sparrow*. This was to become the first of the Weybridge Sailing Club Monologues. So, thank you Martin.

By the same author

The Apollinarian Christologies: a study of the writings of Apollinarius of Laodicea, London, Hamley King Publishing 2011.